GETTING A JOB IN
THE LEGAL
PROFESSION

KATHY FURGANG

Published in 2017 by The Rosen Publishing Group, Inc.
29 East 21st Street, New York, NY 10010

Copyright © 2017 by The Rosen Publishing Group, Inc.

First Edition

Library of Congress Cataloging-in-Publication Data

Names: Furgang, Kathy, author.
Title: Getting a job in the legal profession / Kathy Furgang.
Description: First edition. | New York : Rosen Publishing, 2017. | Series:
 Job basics, getting the job you need | Includes bibliographical references
 and index.
Identifiers: LCCN 2016006445 | ISBN 9781477785621 (library bound)
Subjects: LCSH: Law—Vocational guidance—United States—Juvenile literature.
Classification: LCC KF297 .F865 2016 | DDC 340.023/73—dc23
LC record available at http://lccn.loc.gov/2016006445

Manufactured in China

CONTENTS

INTRODUCTION

Cecile exited the elevator on the 34th floor of the Manhattan skyscraper. The butterflies in her stomach quickly settled down, and her nerves turned to excitement. It was the first day on the job as a paralegal intern in a small law firm. She was wearing her sharpest suit and felt ready for the day.

Cecile had always been interested in law, but knew she might not have the time, money, or stamina to go through law school. Her mother had suggested that becoming a paralegal was a good way to explore the field of law to see if she liked it. Cecile took a certification course and is ready to finish it with a great internship opportunity. She would be learning on-the-job, in a real law environment. She would not be "thrown to the wolves" by lawyers who expect her to research, write a report, or advice people immediately. She was excited to be able to work with a mentor who could teach her the ins and outs of research and litigation.

Cecile was excited because there was so much to learn. There are so many different fields of law and jobs available that a person at any level of education can find a place in the legal field. After taking courses to become a paralegal, Cecile felt ready to tackle the internship.

When she met her mentor, she shook her hand and went on a tour of the offices. She knew that she had to remain professional with everything she did. The law profession requires its employees to be more professional and formal

Courthouses are one of the most recognizable symbols of the legal profession. They are where many legal decisions are made by judges and juries based on the legal arguments of attorneys.

than most other professions, and she was determined not to disappoint her new bosses. She wanted to help give the impression to new clients that they had chosen a respectable and well-established firm. After all, people come to law firms when they need help or advice—sometimes in matters affecting life or death. The firm they choose will be important to them.

Cecile's feelings about her first day are typical of people just starting out in a career in law. Getting there takes some research to figure out the options. It can take some serious academic effort and focus. Finding jobs—researching the right places to apply, crafting resumes, and interviewing—can be both challenging, yet fulfilling.

Someone like Cecile may decide that she likes her work as a paralegal so much that it inspires her to take an even bigger step: she can apply to go law school and become a lawyer. There are countless specialties she can focus on, in both public service and private practices. She can even channel her efforts to eventually become judge—the highest honor and position in the field of law.

There are an amazing number of options available to people who are interested in a legal career. Cecile's career path is just one of many open to anyone who chooses to explore the field of law.

CHAPTER ONE

Surveying the Field: The Legal Landscape

T he first step in exploring the field of law is to become familiar with what is available and the jobs that people can have. Even if you are not sure whether you want to become a lawyer or just work in the field, it's helpful to know how the field of law breaks down into different specialties, disciplines, and types of law. Within each specialty, someone can be a lawyer, paralegal, legal assistant, file clerk, or other law professional.

Fields of Law

There are a vast number of choices in the field of law. Students considering what to lean toward should review the choices and think about what interests them most. Maintaining a high interest level in your chosen field of work is important. It can be difficult to go to work each day to a job that you struggle to stay interested in. The following sub-categories of law are among the most widely practiced.

Criminal Law

Criminal law involves the process of punishment of those who commit crimes. A lawyer may choose to defend the rights of the person accused of the crime, or the rights of the person against whom the crime was committed. Because laws are set by the government, criminal law cases are prosecuted by the government. It is the lawyer's job to either prove that a person committed the crime or to defend a client who may have been unfairly accused of a crime.

Corporate and Securities Law

Corporate law is a division of the law field that studies how parts of a business interact with each other and makes sure they do so in accordance with laws. The relationship between corporate directors and their shareholders is important in corporate law. Corporate lawyers also handle any problems between consumers or community members. Even environmental problems that the corporation

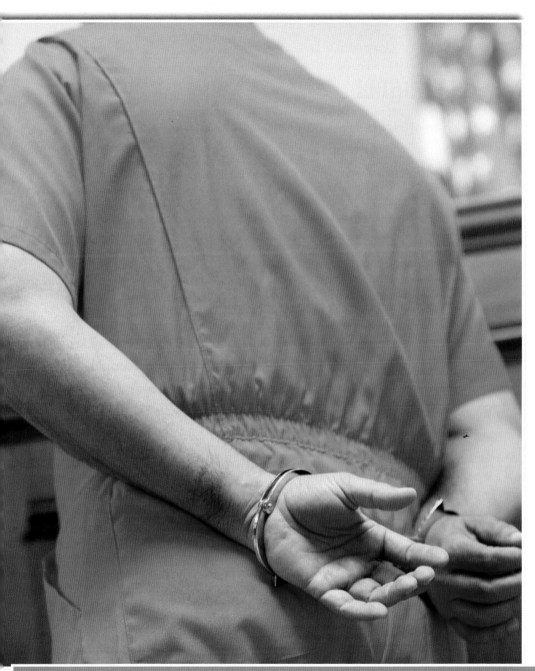

Many areas of law overlap. For example, a corporate and securities lawyer may be involved in a criminal case with his or her client.

may be involved in are handled and defended under the umbrella of corporate law.

Civil Rights

With civil rights law, the rights of the individual are upheld. If a person feels that their government-granted rights have been violated, a civil rights lawyer can consider the case. Civil rights lawyers might go against a corporation, and some criminal cases might overlap into the area of civil rights. In this case, different legal cases can be tried in these different areas of law.

Labor and Employment

Labor law is often called employment law. This type of law field is concerned with the relationship between employers and employees. This involves what the employer is legally obligated to provide for the employee, and what the employee's rights are in the job. Some issues covered in this type of law include safety issues, benefits, and problems of pay or harassment in the workplace.

Environmental

The concerns of the environmental field of law are that environmental regulations are followed. Some environmental lawyers defend people who might have been affected by pollution or other environmental problems. Their goal is to protect the environment and to make sure it is properly regulated. This may mean prosecuting individuals or businesses that do not protect endangered plants or animals.

Family Law

A family lawyer deals with matters between families and family members. This can include adoption laws, or even matters concerning child abuse or child abduction. Family law also concerns civil unions and domestic partnerships. A specialty of family law can include divorce law.

Immigration

A specialist in immigration law is very familiar with the federal laws about who can enter the country, for what reason, and for how long. Immigration lawyers also help people follow the right steps in becoming a citizen. Immigration law may overlap into areas such as family law or criminal law if the people being defended have a criminal case or a family issue that relates to the person's legal status in the country.

Real Estate Law

Lawyers involved in real estate law may have a specialty, such as residential real estate or commercial real estate. They can help people follow or interpret laws about buying or selling real estate. They may also be able to help people follow the laws involved in buying or selling property to be developed.

Tax Law

A tax lawyer is involved in the process of explaining and interpreting taxes. This may be on the federal, state, or local level. Tax lawyers help determine what type of taxes are owed for different reasons. They may work closely with accountants, who specialize in taxes.

Estate Law

This type of lawyer works to help an individual deal with the net worth of their entire estate. An estate is all the money and property owned by a person. This is useful especially when someone is preparing to leave their property to others after their death. Estate lawyers can help people plan wills. They can also help with issues of personal bankruptcy or help someone deal with large changes in the value of their personal estate.

Sports/Entertainment

Lawyers who specialize in sports or entertainment may be able to help both professionals and amateurs in the sports and entertainment fields. They are often involved in negotiating contracts and dealing with publicity issues on the behalf of their clients.

Copyright Law

The field of copyright law protects authors of original works. Federal copyright laws ensure that the authors of literary, dramatic, or any artistic or musical work are considered the owners of these works. Copyrights are applied for, not automatically granted by creating a work. The guidance of lawyers who specialize in this field can help clients who are accused of violating these laws or clients who think others have violated their copyrights.

Real estate law is one of the most common specialties in the legal profession. A lawyer can protect clients from legal problems surrounding their mortgages or rental lease agreements.

International Law

Federal laws differ from nation to nation, so some lawyers specialize in how treaties between nations are established and carried out. Specialization in international law can require knowledge of other languages, cultures, customs, and laws.

Common Jobs in the Legal Profession

When we think of jobs in the legal profession, a lawyer most likely springs to mind first. Lawyers do take up a large portion of the law profession, and there are an wide array of niches that lawyers can practice within. But there are other career paths in the legal profession that require different skill sets and training, and are miles apart when it comes to their day-to-day responsibilities and tasks.

In March 2015, the family of late singer and songwriter Marvin Gaye won $7.4 million in damages for copyright infringement from Pharrell Williams and Robin Thicke, who were found guilty of stealing portions of one of Gaye's songs.

Lawyer

The job description of a lawyer would be longer than the length of this book. The short explanation is that they represent clients who hire them for their legal assistance and advice. Providing that assistance and advice involves an extremely long list of tasks. They prepare documents, they do research, they explain laws, and they question their clients to learn more about their circumstances. The list goes on and on. The lawyer's responsibilities are so vast, in fact, that there are other people in other roles who have the sole responsibility of helping lawyers to fulfill their responsibilities.

Lawyers typically are the most highly educated and trained of any staff at a law firm. They have gone to school for the longest amount of time and earned a difficult graduate degree. Most other people in a law firm do not have law degrees, but they can help run the office and make cases run smoothly. A paralegal is one example of a person who can take on some of the responsibilities of a lawyer to ease the workload.

Paralegal

Although a paralegal performs support work in the legal field, a paralegal is not an assistant to a lawyer. There are many things a paralegal is trained to do legally, according to their certification, which can be done in the absence of a lawyer. That includes drafting legal documents such as contracts, pleas, subpoenas, and legal briefs.

Paralegals do handle administrative work, help schedule attorney's times, and make travel arrangements. They might also interview clients, take notes, and summarize the

Lawyers and paralegals spend a lot of time researching previous court cases to prepare for their own cases. Without the aid of paralegals, most law offices could not run smoothly and efficiently.

information for the attorney. They even do a lot of legal research and may present that research to the attorney or attorneys on the case.

A paralegal often has a very hands-on relationship with the clients, and may have more frequent contact with the client than a lawyer does. Paralegals must have a very professional manner when dealing with clients. They must also have sharp written and verbal skills. These are skills that someone can improve over time, but they are also needed to a certain extent before a person gets hired for a job.

Legal professionals often work in teams, with several lawyers and paralegals taking care of different aspects of a case. This allows for people to focus on a particular task throughout the case and to be available to clients throughout the case in reliable and predictable ways.

Going the Distance: Becoming a Judge

What can a person expect after many years of experience in the law profession? One goal to strive for is to become a judge. A judge is a public official who is appointed by the government to decide on court cases. They hear the entire case from both sides, and they make the important concluding decision. In some cases, that decision is whether a case has been proven to the court. In other cases, in which a jury decides that someone is guilty, the judge decides on the punishment. A judge is considered the most respected person in the legal field. Judges must be impartial and know the law in great detail.

OTHER LEGAL POSITIONS

Within the field of law, there are many jobs available for people with a wide variety of training.

Professions that Do Not Require a Legal Degree:

- File clerks perform general office work, especially regarding the filing and maintenance of records.
- Court reporters work in the courtroom to keep an official record of the proceedings. This person may also be called a court stenographer, named for the transcribing machine that is used to make official transcripts of the cases.
- Court interpreters help convert speech or sign language in a courtroom or other legal setting. Court interpreters are needed in order for people who do not speak English to take part in the case.
- Legal analysts provide assistance to attorneys and legal teams.

Professions that Require a Legal Degree:

- Litigation support consultants are experienced attorneys who can provide expert advice to attorneys on a case. They may work for a firm or be hired independently.
- Trial consultants are available for preparing and carrying out a trial. These are also experienced attorneys who can lend their knowledge to benefit others in their firm.
- Jurists are experts in the field of law. They are often legal scholars who are very familiar with the history of landmark cases and can provide insight into legal issues. Some jurists are writers who analyze law in journals or books.
- Mediators or arbitrators are independent legal professionals who are assigned to settle a dispute between parties. This person may sometimes be a judge.
- Jury consultants work together with attorneys to choose the best jury possible for a trial.
- Electronic discovery experts hold a relatively new position in the law field. They help firms keep up-to-date with new technologies. They also help firms store and retrieve digital information. These specialists are usually attorneys who know both the technology and the law required to do the job effectively.

Judges serve in every courthouse throughout the country. They often do their own research on a case in addition to hearing lawyers present arguments in order to help form an opinion or make a decision.

The Supreme Court is the highest court in the United States, and it is the highest honor to be appointed to this position by the president of the United States. The court decides some of the most important cases facing the nation. It is important to note that each Supreme Court judge started on the same path that many of the future legal professionals reading this book started on.

Laying the Educational Foundation

J ust as there are many options for work in the legal field, there are also many educational requirements for those jobs. It can seem confusing at times, but there are ways to break it down into manageable areas. First, break down the jobs based on the educational requirements. While going to law school to become an attorney will add years to your career path, there are some jobs that only require a certificate. They do not even require a high school degree, although a high school diploma will always offer you an advantage in the workforce.

Think About the Options

Before deciding what to focus on or what career to choose, ask yourself if you plan on continuing your education in the traditional tract. That means a high school diploma, then a college degree, and possibly post-graduate work. This is an important consideration, because a person in college might have the time or opportunity to explore courses related to law. This can help a person to choose whether the field of law is right for him or her. However, not everyone's career paths are straight and narrow. People may not become interested in law until later in life, or they may not have the time or money to explore such options while in school. But if you plan to go to college, choose one that has a variety of classes related to law and the practice of law.

No matter what section of the law profession you pursue, it will likely mean studying for classes, tests, or certifications. Exams during law school and the bar examination afterward require a tremendous amount of dedication.

Even if a person is not planning to go through a bachelor's program, it is important to search the schools in your area to see if any law courses can be taken without the connection to a major or a degree program. This can give a sense of what the field is like. The workload in the course can provide a clue about what the profession may be like and what is expected of students pursuing law.

Certificate Programs

Attending college may not be necessary at all for people pursuing some law professions. For example, the job of a legal assistant, paralegal, court stenographer, file clerk, court stenographer, or legal analyst can be open to someone very quickly if he or she does some research. In many cases, just a certification is required for someone to get started. Each school is different and has different requirements for students. That means you must research schools located near you and see what they have to offer.

One benefit of a certificate program is that the student can be more directed in his or her career path and get there earlier than someone who is working on a college degree. The classes are more directed and focused on a career path. It is assumed that someone who takes the certificate program knows what he or she wants to do. The certification will help the student reach his or her goals faster because it is focused.

For example, a typical certification program for a legal assistant may consist of six required courses and three electives. Check for timing requirements as you search for schools. Many will require that the courses be completed within a two-year period. Also check for any prerequisites or required

Working as a court stenographer usually requires certification. It can be a demanding but interesting job to have.

prior skills. For example, legal assistants must do a lot of typing as part of their job, and may be assumed that students entering the classes should already know how to type at a certain speed. The courses are not meant to teach the basics of typing, but to help students use those skills to become effective legal assistants.

Be on the lookout for schools that offer combined certificates. For example, you may be able to have some of your required courses for a legal assistant certificate count toward a certificate in legal studies as well. While it may cost a bit more to have double certification, there may be more options available to you when you begin searching for a job.

Typical courses required for a legal assistant certificate include an introduction to law, drafting contracts, legal research and writing, litigation, bookkeeping, budgeting, accounting, and computer courses such as Microsoft Excel.

A certification in Legal Studies might help someone who is

Law schools often have large libraries of legal documents for students to use in their studies. Each subsection of the law has many volumes covering decades of case law and precedents.

considering becoming a paralegal or possibly going to law school. In addition to the administrative courses, a legal studies program offers courses about different law specialties, such as criminal law, corporate law, or family law.

Keep in mind that not all law firms may require that a person have a certification to start working in their firm. However, when someone has a certification, they have an advantage over someone who is not certified.

Exploring Law School Options

Going to law school is a big decision for anyone. All but the lowest ranked law programs are relatively expensive. Hence, a legal education is a big investment, More importantly, it is often one of the biggest academic challenges of any person's academic career. The sheer amount of reading, memorization, and work can be intimidating. However, the payoff of becoming a lawyer can be immense, and many attorneys look back and admit their decision was one of the best they ever made.

If you are considering law school in the future, start by working hard and succeeding as much as you can during the time you are earning your bachelor's degree. A bachelor's degree, or four-year college, is a requirement for entry into law school. The entry into most law schools is very competitive, so do your best and get grades as high as you can. Law schools look for students with high grade point averages and who show leadership qualities with the clubs and activities they take part in at college.

Although many students may think that being a pre-law major is the best choice for a major as an undergraduate, that is not always the case. Law schools look for students who have a strong ability to think abstractly and analytically.

GETTING READY FOR SCHOOL

Whether you are interested in getting a Juris Doctor degree or simply getting a certificate, thorough research will help you make the right decision. First, consider your finances and whether you will need to take a loan. Law school is notoriously expensive, but pays off in the long run financially depending on which subset of law you end up practicing.

On the other hand, some certifications can be quite reasonable and lead to good job opportunities. Schedule time to visit schools and ask questions about their programs. Research the application deadlines, fees, and requirements. Will you need to write an essay? Do you need recommendations from teachers or other professionals? Keep track of application deadlines and be sure to submit the materials on time. Keep in mind that the entire process may take many months. The LSAT tests are only given four times per year, and schools have very specific deadlines only one time per year. It can take a lot of planning and hard work to meet these dates.

Philosophy, journalism, and economics majors are often considered good candidates for law school, especially from schools that do not offer pre-law programs.

Before applying to law school, prospective students must take the Law School Admission Test (LSAT). This test is similar to the SAT that students take before applying to colleges. The LSAT is a standardized test that measures critical thinking and reasoning skills. It measures the student's ability to think analytically about readings. Most questions are multiple choice, and a timed writing response is required.

The LSAT is offered four times a year at different testing centers around the world. Classes are offered to help students prepare for the test and take practice exams. Applying

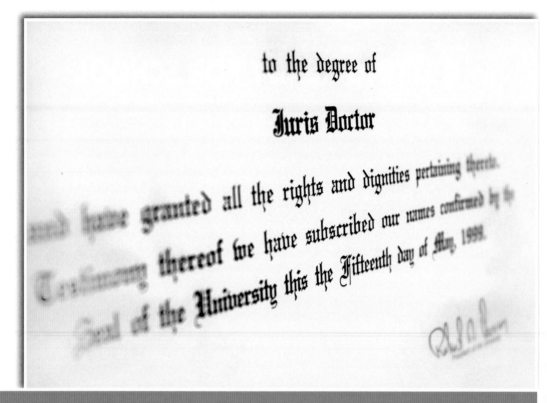

to the degree of

Juris Doctor

and have granted all the rights and dignities pertaining thereto. Testimony thereof we have subscribed our names confirmed by the seal of the University this the Fifteenth day of May, 1999.

Earning a Juris Doctor (J.D.) degree requires passing the bar exam. Many law school graduates take the test multiple times before they pass it and can therefore practice law in a particular state.

to schools is the next step in the process of heading to law school. This can include a process of visiting schools, filling out applications, and paying fees to apply.

Law school usually involves a three-year course of study that results in a Juris Doctor (J.D.) degree. Students are expected to work through the courses on a full-time basis and not at their own pace, setting their own schedule.

After going through the program, the last step is to pass a test called the bar exam. Bar exams differ by region, such as by state or country. The test determines whether a candidate is qualified to practice law in that region. A person must plan to study for and take the bar exam for the area in which they plan to practice law.

Although many students go directly into law school after earning their undergraduate degree, many do not. A person can work for years as a paralegal or legal assistant and then decide they would like to pursue a Juris Doctor degree. People can attend law school during any time in their lives. In fact, someone who gets working experience in a law firm before attending law school may be better able to analyze cases they study at school. A person's real-life work experiences can make them a better law student and lawyer later in life.

Researching Jobs

Finding a job in the law field may seem like a daunting task. However, it does not have to be that way. There are plenty of ways that people can find jobs in the legal profession. If you are still in school, you may even have an advantage over people who are not. Guidance offices are a great place to start your research. A guidance office often has files of resources that students can use to help them in their search.

For example, local law offices that like to use young people or that offer internships for school credit may contact local high schools and colleges. A description of the opportunity will likely be available for students to read. Guidance counselors can help set up interviews, provide school records, and guide the student through the process.

For a person trying to find a job in the law profession without the help of a school, there are plenty of online sources available.

Online Tools

Anyone searching for a job in law can find easy access to lots of information online. Start your journey in the research phase. Look on employment recruitment websites dedicated to legal professionals, such as Lawmatch. There you can get an idea of the jobs available simply by looking at the job titles that are being advertised. You will find everything from assistant secretary positions to corporate counsel attorneys. The jobs can be sorted by state, or global area, as well as the practice setting or specialty. The job functions can also be sorted by the years of experience needed to do the jobs. Categories include entry level, support staff, law student, recent graduate, and everything from managerial to administrative.

Guidance counselors may be able to help students set up interviews, work on their resumes, or find jobs.

Becoming familiar with the job descriptions and qualification requirements of jobs you are interested in can be very informative. You may find that the type of position you want requires a lot more training and experience than you had expected. Or, you may find that you are already qualified for a job you thought would take you years to land.

Websites such as Lawmatch also allow job seekers to post their resumes to the website so that employers can review them. This is helpful when employers have not yet found an applicant they like. They can search through the resumes of people they know are interested in law and find the person they think suits them best.

Compare these job listings to those on general job search websites such as Indeed or CareerBuilder. You may find law jobs advertised in unexpected places. Online newspapers also have job listings, so don't forget about those. Especially consider your local newspaper's online job

Teachers can serve as mentors for students. If you establish a good rapport with a teacher or professor, make it known you are interested in finding out about employment opportunities.

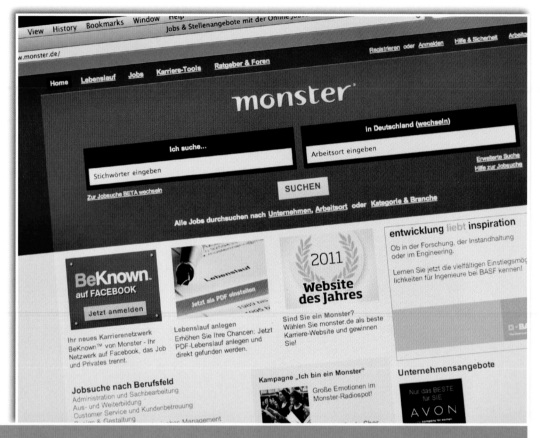

Online job sites are a great source for finding work opportunities in a specific field. They allow the seeker to narrow down jobs and openings in a particular geographic area.

listings because those jobs will likely be in your own area and easy to get to.

As you apply for jobs, be sure to take note of any qualifications for the job and any degrees or tests that are required. It is considered unprofessional to apply for jobs that you are not qualified for. That sends a message to employers that you did not read their job post carefully and are not taking them seriously as a candidate.

You may see a dream job posted on a website, but if you do not have the qualifications the employer is looking for, you will likely have difficulty pulling through and doing the work that is expected of you. Someone who is just starting out in the business should have the opportunity to learn and explore. Being overwhelmed with a job that is too difficult can turn someone off to a field that might otherwise have been a great match.

Internships

Internships are possibly one of the most useful experiences that a young student can participate in. Many internships are offered for credit. A paralegal or law studies certificate program might even require an internship as part of the course load. Internships offer students a chance to learn how a company is structured. This gives new workers a great overview of possible jobs to pursue. Some interns move from department to department so they can be exposed to different aspects of the field. In a large law firm, an intern might spend time in the contracts department for a week or two, then move to the corporate or copyright departments. This is a great opportunity for someone who is just starting out. They might spend time watching attorneys argue, or litigate, in the courtroom.

Another valuable thing about internships is that they are often assigned to a mentor who can help to guide them in their early career. Mentorships have proven to be a great way for professionals to help their careers. Mentors are available when employees have questions or need advice about the job. They can help make their mentees aware of job opportunities within the company or recommend them for certain jobs.

A mentor can really help to kick-start a person's career. As early as high school, an internship and mentor can provide a great example of how the legal field works, what is expected of employees in terms of dress, behavior, and dedication to the job. That experience is usually directed through the efforts of a mentor who is more established in the field and can explain it to a person just starting out.

Using Mentors Throughout Your Career

A mentor is not someone to just leave behind once an internship is over. If a person takes care and planning, the professional relationship with a mentor can last a person's entire career. When looking for a future job opening, a mentor can provide a great recommendation that can mean the difference between getting a job and not getting it. If two applicants apply for a job and are equally qualified in their academic career, a prospective employer will have to look deeper to decide who should be hired. The candidate who has gone through an internship experience can really stand out to an employer. A mentor who can describe the student's performance on that internship can set the prospective employee above the rest. In the eyes of many employers, internships count for on-the-job-training, and mentors show that the student has been set on the right track in the professional world.

Although students often forget about their mentors as they grow older and develop their own career, it is wise to

BUILDING A GREAT RESUME

A resume is just one piece of paper, but it's an extremely important one that can mean the difference between getting a job and not getting a job. Be sure to get assistance with your resume from a teacher or guidance counselor. Once you have an internship, show your resume to a mentor to help you improve it. A resume should include the details about you that make you a good candidate for a job. You must list your educational experience and your job experience. Include brief descriptions of the tasks that you did for each job.

If there is a way to direct your resume toward a law job you are looking for, be sure to do that. For example, court stenographers must know how to type, so list the number of words per minute that you are able to type if you are looking for a job as a court stenographer. Court interpreters must know other languages. If you are searching for this type of experience, definitely list all of the languages you know, and indicate whether you are fluent in any of them. Working for a law journal may require experience in writing. Any experience working on a school newspaper would help for someone interested in work at a law journal. In fact, any writing experience is useful to list on a resume because law offices require employees to communicate well.

Keep your resume to one page, if possible, so employers can quickly review them. Include your most up-to-date personal information including address, phone number, and email address so that you can be contacted quickly and easily.

keep in touch with your mentor. That person will be a great source as you continue to look for jobs in the future. Even when you are more experienced and may become a mentor yourself, it still helps to have someone who can recall details about your work ethic.

A teacher or mentor can help by both writing recommendations and helping you perfect your resume.

Getting Recommendations

As soon as you think about your job search in the law profession, think of a person who can be called on to provide a good recommendation about you. For someone who does not have a mentor in the field, a teacher will be a great substitute. Try to choose a teacher who teaches a subject that requires critical or abstract thinking, such as Writing, English, Social Studies, or Science. Choose the teacher that you have the best relationship with and who you think would say the best things about you.

Teachers are used to writing recommendations for students, so don't worry about bothering them with a favor. A good recommendation can be very helpful when a prospective employer wonders if you can do the job. Have that recommendation ready for if and when it is requested.

Gearing Up to Land the Job

O nce you have researched the law profession or worked in it for a while, you may decide that you want to become certified to do a particular task. This will help you focus your career and land the job you want. But there are things to find out before you proceed. Create a path for yourself and stick to it.

Figuring Out What You Need

Find out if the job you want requires a certification and what is needed to get that certification. For example, a paralegal certificate program is for people who hold an associate's degree or bachelor's degree. But don't automatically worry if you don't meet that requirement. Some programs may allow students who do not have a higher degree if they have had prior work experience at a law firm. It helps to call and talk to someone at the school to see if their requirements are flexible. Continuing to search for schools and programs that meet your needs can pay off in the end. If you're searching for a stenographer's certification and you can't find one, call a school and ask for a recommendation. The law department of a college or university can be a great resource not only for students who go there, but for prospective students who are shopping around for a certification program to meet their needs.

Court stenography is a specialty in the legal profession. The steno machine, pictured here, is the primary tool for stenographers. Nowadays, software and other tools assist stenographers in their work.

Certification Programs

There are many certification programs that can prepare someone for the law profession. For example, the National Court Reporters Association has about a dozen certifications that thousands of court reporters around the country have taken. They have their own certification test centers, and having a certification from them provides a useful tool in landing a job.

The National Center for State Courts (NCSC) provides resources for people interested in becoming court interpreters. Because the job requires communicating in different languages, written and oral exams are required for certification. Check the website of the NCSC for resources and self-assessment tools to help prepare you for certification courses and exams.

Community colleges may also offer certification courses for various court and legal jobs. People interested in becoming court clerks, or legal secretaries can find courses at a community college that may be associated with your county court system and offer internships or other opportunities students may not be familiar with.

Because it takes so much time and effort, remember that you may not have to become certified to work in the legal field in order to get a job. For example, you may be able to be hired as a paralegal and trained on the job. That would save you time and money in your career path. However, realize that someone who is certified can be your competition for the job. That candidate may look more attractive to an employer because of the certification. But you may make an agreement with your employer that you will sign up for a certification program as soon as you get hired. This can be an

Interpreters play an important role in the legal process by helping clients communicate with lawyers, judges, and other people involved in their case. Such jobs are sure to grow in number as the United States grows more diverse.

agreement that you are willing to work hard and earn the certification if they are willing to give you a chance on the job.

Study Methods

Studying for law certification classes and exams can be a stressful thing, but there are several methods to help people get over the anxiety and not have to face the problem alone. Many students both studying to be in the law profession as well as many other professions have used one or more of these useful study tips.

Joining Study Groups

The community college or school that offers the certification may have an opportunity to sign up for study groups that can get people together to review what they learned and review for the tests. This can be a good opportunity for someone who might be struggling with a few things and can benefit from a review.

Study groups are also good for people who like to study by talking with people and working through the content they learned with peers. Study groups are not for everyone, but they can certainly help get people together and talking about what they have learned. There are so many law cases that students must familiarize themselves with that it can be a good idea for students to put their heads together. If someone knows about one case and a partner in a study group knows of another similar case, the group can build an argument for or against something to use in an oral or written report. This is how lawyers work as they prepare for litigation, so it is a good idea to get used to working in groups as you are learning.

Similarly, students studying different law specialties may benefit from studying together because they can give each other a different perspective on a particular case or problem they are asked to approach in class.

Study Guides

When preparing for standardized exams such as the LSAT, there are many study guides available. They provide students with sample tests that can be used to help them become familiar with the type, structure, and length of each section.

Study tips and test-taking strategies are also provided in most test prep guides.

Students who earn an undergraduate degree have likely taken the SAT or other standardized test. The LSAT is similar in its structure, but it is a much more rigorous test because it calls on students to be analytical and think in an abstract way. There's no need to get nervous about the test, however. Taking the LSAT is a good experience, and a good preparation for the rigorous course load that students will face if they decide to go to law school.

Standardized tests like the LSAT are one of the criteria by which prospective students are chosen by law schools. The most prestigious and expensive schools pick among the highest scorers and students with the highest GPAs.

MAKE A BUDGET

Keep in mind that every study guide, test preparation course, school application, and certification test costs money. Keep this in mind as you prepare and set goals for the future. Keep a list of possible expenses that you will need to lay down for your test preparation and the test fee itself. Whenever possible, use library resources to help you. Some colleges have law libraries with excellent resources for students. You may be able to cut some expenses by using test prep books or taking sample LSAT tests from a library. Then do the same if you plan to apply to law schools. Make a list of the application fees for each school, and be sure you can afford to pay for your top picks before beginning the process.

Test Prep Classes

For students who don't do well studying from guidebooks by themselves, a test prep class may be a good alternative. Teachers may be able to guide students through sample questions and model the thought process the student should be going through to choose the answer.

Teachers are often helpful, also, in preparing students to take the written part of a standardized test. Throughout the test prep class, the teacher can assign several writing assignments that mimic the writing task on the LSAT. Then the teacher can review the responses and give students feedback that can be incorporated before they take the real test.

Test prep classes can also be beneficial because they give students a chance to meet students who may have taken the test multiple times. Students can network and discuss what the test was like and what can be expected in terms of difficulty.

The Bar Exam

The bar exam is the ultimate test of strength for the law student, and for any student, for that matter. Many students must take the bar exam several times before they pass—that's how difficult the test is. It takes full-time dedication to studying and preparing for the test.

Each state has a different test, and they vary in their difficulty level. For example, California has one of the most

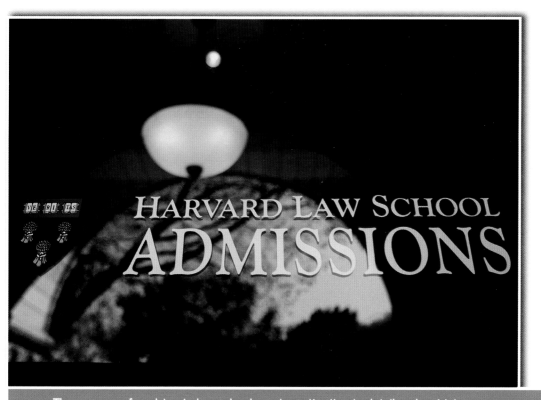

HARVARD LAW SCHOOL
ADMISSIONS

The process of applying to law school requires attention to detail and a strict adherence to deadlines. Harvard Law School is often ranked at or near the top of the most competitive schools to get into.

rigorous bar exams. It involves 18 hours of testing over a span of three days. The overall number of students who pass it is just around 72 percent. Students who really want to practice law in California may be forced to take the test several times until they pass. That means studying over and over again for the 18 hours of testing.

Law students also have an option of taking a Multistate Bar Examination (MBE), which can qualify someone to practice law in various areas around the United States and its territories. Only Louisiana does not administer the test, due to its state's own civil law system. The test is based on several areas of law, such as constitutional, criminal, family, real estate, and business law. A person taking the test needs a wide knowledge of each area and the ability to analyze cases in each specialty.

Anyone considering law school should not be scared off by the idea of taking the bar exam, but they should be aware that it is the final challenge to becoming a practicing attorney.

CHAPTER FIVE

The Interview

A job interview at a law firm can be intimidating, whether you are applying for a job as a court clerk or as an attorney. There are many ways to prepare for a job interview and make it as successful as possible. The way you dress and carry yourself are important, as are the things you say and discuss. Knowing how to handle yourself on a job interview can pay off and provide you with the career you have been waiting to break into.

Scheduling the Interview

You are so excited to get that phone call. You've been called to an interview with that law firm you were so excited to apply with. After speaking politely with them on the phone to thank them for the opportunity to meet with you, it's time to schedule the interview. Be ready with a good response to that important question: When is the best time for you?

Think about your normal schedule and when you are usually at your best. If you are a morning person, definitely make the interview when you will be able to think and perform at your best. Morning interviews are also good because they leave you with the rest of your day worry-free. They also take

Be sure to have a backup transportation plan on days when you have a job interview. Losing a coveted position due to a flat tire is the last thing you want to happen.

part at times when the firm has not yet been able to fall behind on their daily schedule, so you are more likely to be seen on time if you schedule a morning interview.

Think of your transportation as well, however. If you will need a ride and that will only be available in the afternoon, that will be an important part of your scheduling plans. Whatever you choose, be prompt so that you do not leave people waiting for you. The interview is the employer's first impression of you, so you want to give them every reason to have a good impression of you.

Dressing the Part

If you're wondering what the best thing to wear to an interview at a law firm or courthouse is, think formal. The law profession is one of the most formal and conservative in attire, so dress the part as well as you can. That does not mean that you should break the bank trying to dress yourself like an accomplished lawyer, but be neat and formal. Men should wear a suit, and women should wear formal business attire as well.

It is understood that court stenographers, secretaries, and file clerks or court clerks may not be able to afford very expensive attire. However, the dress should be as neat and conservative as possible. The interviewee's attire shows that he or she is serious about the job and ready to reflect the firm or court's image to the public.

The type of law being practiced in a certain office can also affect the way an interviewee dresses. It may not be appropriate for a civil rights lawyer or someone who defends the poor to wear flashy attire. Conservative but simple dress is most appropriate way to appear for an interview at a firm that deals with public defense.

Being Prepared

Before you go to the interview, spend some time writing down notes. Think about the typical things you will be asked: Why do you want to be a court stenographer? How did you hear about our firm? Why are you interested in litigation? What do you think you have to offer our team of lawyers?

Think of the answers to each of these questions, and practice answering them out loud. It may not be as easy as it seems to answer questions about yourself and your goals. But the more articulate you can be, the better an impression you will make on the firm.

Stenographers or file clerks may not be expected to be as sophisticated in interviews as someone interviewing for a job as a courtroom litigator, but any job candidate should be as responsive and articulate as possible in an interview. Law is a field in which communication is very important.

Attorneys specializing in litigation or arbitration should be highly articulate. Those candidates hoping for a chance at a court interpreter position will also need to be well spoken and a good interview candidate. Someone who is looking for a job in which they communicate with others will have a better chance of landing one if they can express themselves.

The law is a conservative field. Always dress professionally for a job interview, especially for a job as an attorney.

Employment agencies sometimes offer chances for people to practice interviewing. Signing up with an agency can help keep an eye out for new work opportunities, but you also might be able to take advantage of interviewing dry runs. Just

Be well-spoken and confident in your interview, without being arrogant. Practicing can help you sharpen your interviewing skills. These abilites reflect directly on your potential as a lawyer or other worker in the legal field.

the process of signing up with an employment agency can give you an opportunity to interview with the recruiters. They are trained to give interview tips, and they may even have advice on how to improve your resume. If you have an

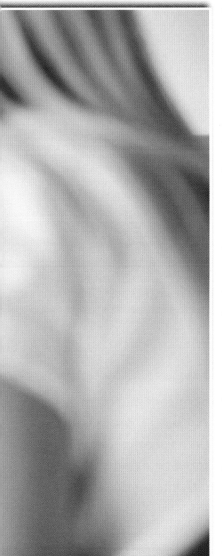

employment or recruitment agency near your home, take advantage of it if you can.

Another way to prepare for an interview is to go with your own list of questions that you would like to ask the interviewer. However, don't go into the interview and ask them all at once. The interviewer will have plenty of information to give you about the firm and the job during the course of the interview. Listen carefully and wait until the end of the interview. If there are any questions from your list that have not yet been addressed, ask them then. Having smart, thoughtful questions is always a plus, especially for a field where workers are supposed to be intellectually curious and engaged.

The Right Amount of Information

The interviewer will give you plenty of information about the job, but part of the process of an interview

A FIVE-YEAR GOAL

One of the most classic interview questions in any profession is, "Where do you see yourself in five years?" For some jobs, this question may be pointless filler. But for many legal positions, it makes you really think about what you want out of a particular job or career track. This question forces the interviewee to think about the future and hopefully come up with a vision of himself or herself rising up in the company, or at least remaining interested in the career path that this job interview could unlock. Remember that there's no right or wrong way to answer this question. However, it might help to think about the answer before going on an interview. It may be helpful to let the interviewer know if you have ambitions to go to law school one day and become an attorney. Or perhaps you have an interest in a particular kind of law, such as family law or copyright law. You might see yourself working in that area of law in five years.

Whatever your five year plan, make it clear that you are flexible and want to learn as much as you can about the law profession within that time. You may be surprised. The interviewer may have a plan about how you might be able to reach your five-year goal at the firm or courthouse. Even if you have not really thought it through or are not sure yet, it is a good idea to prepare something in answer to this question. Prospective bosses prefer drive and ambition to indecision.

is to find out about you. Speak about your academic or other accomplishments, and name the skills that would make you a good legal secretary or court reporter. What computer skills would make you a good electronic discovery expert? What experience with human behavior would make you a good jury consultant?

It's alright, however, to not give information about your private life. That should not be a topic of conversation during your interview, and you are not competing with other candidates based on the personal details of your life. Stick to the

An old trick that can help you is to practice interviewing in the mirror at home.
You can even give yourself a pep talk if necessary.

Even your demeanor while waiting to be called into an interview can reflect on you. Count on the fact that the person at reception may tell your interviewer if you were polite and professional upon arrival.

discussions about the firm or court, the job description, the work environment, and the professional skills that would make you a good match in for the job.

Making a Good Impression

A good job candidate will do more than just list his or her skills. One of the most important parts about making a good impression is showing confidence. This is especially true for someone who wants to become a lawyer, make arguments, and litigate in front of a courtroom. Even court stenographers need to show confidence in an interview. They may have to speak up in a courtroom full of people and ask for clarification or for something to be repeated.

Showing confidence in an interview means making and keeping eye contact with the interviewer. It means shaking hands as a greeting and speaking in a clear and friendly tone. It may seem like common sense, but when people get into an interview they are often nervous. They may not put forth their most confident demeanor. Or, they may be working so hard to cover up their nerves that they forget to shake hands or make eye contact with their interviewer.

CHAPTER SIX

The First Day and Beyond

O nce you have that job you've been looking for, be sure to continue to make a good impression on your employer. Continue to dress appropriately, show up on time, and act professionally. Your employer expects to see that behavior from you not only in the interview, but on the job as well. Your actions as a new employee reflect on you, and you are just meeting many colleagues for the first time. Make those first impressions count. You are forming new professional relationships that may last for years.

Human Resources

New employees should be sure they understand all of the information that was given to them regarding any benefits, vacation days, or sick days they are entitled to. Many companies have human resources departments that specialize in helping new employees become oriented in the job. Take advantage of this department and make sure you understand your employee rights and benefits.

Ask Questions

Even though you got the job you had worked so hard to get, the on-the-job learning curve is only just beginning. As a new employee, however, don't forget to ask questions and make sure you learn your job thoroughly. This will help you to grow as an employee and be able to be a contributing part of the team. Many people feel that asking questions may mean that they were not listening or did not understand something that was said previously. This is not true. Asking questions shows that the person is making an effort to understand something. Asking questions means that the person is taking an interest in the job.

One important question to ask yourself as you are on the job is if you are doing everything you can to do a thorough job. If the answer is yes, you can ask your question to someone else. If you feel comfortable with your workload, it will look good if you take initiative and take it upon yourself to ask a superior if you can take on more responsibility. That kind of behavior can help you get noticed and even get you promoted down the road.

Keep Options Open

Even if you just went through a difficult certification program to get the job you have now, remember that you are never stuck with no options. As long as you are dedicated to your work and can perform your job well, there is no harm in continuing to research other areas of the law profession.

Once you are in the middle of the action and working with clients day-to-day, you may get a sense of what you enjoy most. You might even get a sense of where your talents lie. If you are good at interviewing clients, you may eventually want to move from a job as a paralegal to a prosecutor. If you worked for months as a legal secretary and find criminal cases to be the most interesting ones you work on, you may want to work for an attorney that specializes in criminal law. Keeping your options open to new career possibilities is something that everyone in the law profession should do— whether they have worked in the business for a few months or a few decades.

How to Act on the Job

The field of law has an especially strong need for confidentiality between clients and those who work with them. Some cases that law firms handle involve sensitive issues including violence, crime, divorce, drug use, or difficult problems between corporations or between governments and citizens. The employees who work at the law firms who handle these cases must be aware of client confidentiality and act in a highly ethical way.

Even the legal secretaries, court stenographers, or paralegals must remain very careful about the information they are given. They must not discuss cases outside the law office, and must keep the client's information private at all times.

Ethics is such an important part of a law firm that just one incorrect move can become known to the public and ruin a firm's reputation. An employee who acts unethically can very quickly ruin his or her career path.

As a new hire, be respectful and deferential to senior employees and superiors. Pay your dues and let your work speak for itself, and you will climb the ladder.

An understanding of your clients' circumstances can help you serve them better, as can showing sympathy. The most important thing, of course, is to work hard to represent their interests.

Keep the Clients in Mind

Transparency is an important issue in any law position. Honesty and integrity with clients is one of the most important things to keep in mind when dealing with the public every day. The actions of the law staff affects real people's lives. The work that is put into cases can mean saving someone from going to jail—or it can mean sending someone away to jail as punishment. In criminal cases especially, the lives of clients are sometimes placed in the hands of the law staff. They must do their best to make their case heard and then wish for the best when the jury or judge reaches a decision. This can be stressful work, but it can be rewarding as well.

People in all levels of the legal process work together to help clients and make sure that justice is properly carried out. From the simplest court clerk to the highest judge, every court case is meant to carry out justice. If the court system does not work and justice is not served, clients may do more than wonder what went wrong. They may lose custody of their children. They may be sent to jail for something they did not do. They may be forced to pay fines for something they did not do. There may be no justice for the people who need it.

Doing any work in the legal system requires being thorough and diligent in your work. Sometimes courts appoint lawyers to cases so they can help clients who cannot afford lawyers themselves. These people deserve the same hard work, respect, and dedication as the clients who pay huge fees for legal representation. Shortcomings in the legal system have no place in our society. This is part of the reason why law firms try to have such a clean and spotless reputation.

AN EYE TOWARD THE FUTURE

Some of the jobs in the law industry that do not require extensive education are entry-level jobs. If you work at an entry-level job for a few years, consider whether you would like to go back to school to receive more education. For example, a paralegal may decide to go back to school to become a lawyer, or a lawyer may decide that he or she would eventually one day like to become a judge. Always thinking about the future can help someone stay focused on the career path

Being able to work as part of a team is one of the most important skills a person can bring to a law firm. Many cases are complex and take years to play out, so you may be on a team for a certain case for a long time.

The American legal system was founded on the very basic principles of the nation's constitution. The judicial system's job of interpreting the law has been working for hundreds of years. The system should remain strong enough so that it can work for hundreds more.

Some people choose to become lawyers because the profession pays well. However, the reason people should want to become lawyers and work anywhere in the legal profession is not to make money. It should be to support the constitution and carry out its plan to provide citizens with the justice they deserve. Instead of thinking of the profession as a way to become wealthy, it should be thought of as a way to serve the community.

associate's degree Associate of Arts degree granted by a community or junior college after a two-year course of study.

bachelor's degree Bachelor of Arts degree granted by a college or university after a four-year course of study.

bankruptcy The state of being declared by law to be unable to pay outstanding debts.

certification The state of having received an official document to show that a particular course of study has been completed.

civil law The system of law concerning private matters between members of a community, as opposed to criminal matters.

civil union A union between two individuals that includes legal rights similar to marriage.

copyright A legal recognition given to the creator of a piece of art, music, or literature that grants rights to that person as the owner, including the right to profit from it.

council An individual or group of people who advise and represent the legal affairs of another person.

ethics The moral principles that guide the behavior of a person or group.

Internship A temporary work position meant to train someone in a certain field of work, often for school credit instead of pay.

Juris Doctor A degree awarded to an individual who has successfully completed law school.

litigation The process of taking legal action.

LSAT Law School Admission Test; the test given to grant admission to law school.

MBE Multistate Bar Examination; the bar examination that can be given throughout the United States and its territories to legally practice law.

mentorship A personal and professional relationship between a person learning a trade or craft and the more experienced person who guides him or her.

plea A formal statement of guilt or innocence that a person makes in response to a legal charge against them.

prosecute To go through a legal course of action against a person or organization.

securities Proofs of ownership (once on paper, but now largely digital) of debts and investments, such as a stock or bond.

subpoena A legal document ordering a person to appear in court.

will A legal document with instructions for distributing a person's property or wealth after death.

Federation of Law Societies of Canada
World Exchange Place
1810-45 O'Connor
Ottawa, ON K1P 1A4
Canada
(613) 236-7272
Email: info@flsc.ca
Website: http://flsc.ca
The Federation of Law Societies of Canada is an organiza-
tion that works to unite Canada's 14 law societies so
that provincial and territorial rules and procedures can
serve as positive example of legal governance worldwide.

Law School Admission Council (LSAC)
662 Penn Street
Newtown PA 18940
(215) 968-1001
Email: website-feedback@LSAC.org
Website: http://www.lsac.org/index
The LSAC provides services to people applying to law
school in the United States, Canada, and Australia. It
administers the LSAT and helps students to prepare.

Law Society of Upper Canada
Osgoode Hall, 130 Queen Street West
Toronto, Ontario M5H 2N6
Canada
(800) 668-7380
E-mail: lawsociety@lsuc.on.ca
Website: http://www.lsuc.on.ca

The Law Society of Upper Canada is an organization that
governs the lawyers and paralegals of Ontario and also
provides services and law society events for the public.
National Association for Law Placement (NALP)
1120 19th Street NW, Suite 401
Washington, DC 20036-2405
(202) 835-1001
E-mail: info@nalp.org
Website: http://www.nalp.org/home
The NALP is an organization that provides counseling and
planning for people interested in a legal career. They
recruit law students and lawyers in the United States.

National Center for State Courts (NCSC)
300 Newport Avenue
Williamsburg, VA 23185
(800) 616-6164
Website: http://www.ncsc.org
The National Center for State Courts is an independent,
nonprofit organization dedicated to the improvement of
courts worldwide. It provides research material, com-
parative data, education, and information services to
courts implementing improvements.

National Court Reporters Association (NCRA)
12030 Sunrise Valley Drive
Suite 400
Reston, VA 20191
(800) 272-6272
Email: MSIC@ncrahq.org
Website: http://www.ncra.org

The National Court Reporters Association is an educational resource for people interested in court reporter certification. They help influence laws regarding certification and court reporting requirements.

National Federation of Paralegal Associations
23607 Highway 99, Suite 2-C
Edmonds, WA 98026
(425) 967-0045
E-mail: info@paralegals.org
Website: http://www.paralegals.org
The National Federation of Paralegals Associations helps to increase educational and technological resources for paralegals.

Websites

Because of the changing number of Internet links, Rosen Publishing has developed an online list of websites related to the subject of this book. This site is updated regularly. Please use this link to access this list:
http://www.rosenlinks.com/JOBS/legal

Berk-Seligson, Susan. *The Bilingual Courtroom: Court Interpreters in the Judicial Process*. Chicago, IL: University of Chicago Press, 2012.

Breyer, Stephen. *The Court and the World: American Law and the New Global Realities*. New York: Knopf, 2015.

Farnsworth, Ward. *The Legal Analyst: A Toolkit for Thinking about the Law*. Chicago, IL: University of Chicago Press, 2007.

Feinman, Jay. Law 101: *Everything You Need to Know About American Law*. Oxford, UK: Oxford Univerisity Press, 2014.

Garner, Bryan A. *Legal Writing in Plain English, Second Edition: A Text with Exercises*. Chicago, IL: University of Chicago Press, 2013.

Harr, Scott J. *Careers in Criminal Justice and Related Fields: From Internship to Promotion*. 6th edition. Boston, MA: Wadsworth Publishing, 2009.

Jefferson, Taren. *Paralegal Career: What No One Will Tell You About Paralegal Studies*. Kindle Edition. Seattle, WA: Amazon Digital Services, Inc., 2015.

Leyva, José Luis. *The 1333 Most Frequently Used Legal Terms*. El Paso, TX: Idea Editorial, 2012.

Miller, Robert H. *Law School Confidential: A Complete Guide to the Law School Experience: By Students, for Students*. New York: St. Martins Griffin, 2011.

Miller, Roger LeRoy. *Paralegal Today: The Legal Team at Work*. Clifton Park, NY: Delmar Cengage Learning, 2013.

National Association of Law Placement (NALP). *Official Guide to Legal Specialties* (Career Guides). Gilbert, 2008.

Okrent, Cathy J. *Legal Terminology for Transcription and Court Reporting*. Clifton Park, NY: Cengage Learning, 2008.

"Court Reporters." Occupational Outlook Handbook. Bureau of Labor Statistics. Retrieved January 12, 2016 (http://www.bls.gov/ooh/legal/court-reporters.htm).

Deeb, George. "The Importance of Mentors, and Where to Find Them." Forbes.com, January 30, 2015. Retrieved January 15, 2016 (http://www.forbes.com/sites/georgedeeb/2015/01/30/the-importance-of-mentors-where-to-find-them/#2715e4857a0b7bb322765aa6).

"Fields of Law." Law Careers Advising. Brown University. Retrieved January 10, 2016 (http://www.brown.edu/academics/college/advising/law-school/fields-law/fields-law).

"Legal Assistant" Continuing Education at Hunter. Hunter College. Retrieved January 12, 2016 (http://www.hunter.cuny.edu/ce/certificates/legal-certificates/legal-Assistant).

"Legal Studies" Continuing Education at Hunter. Hunter College. Retrieved January 12, 2016 (http://www.hunter.cuny.edu/ce/certificates/legal-certificates/legal-studies/?searchterm=legal%20studies).

"NCRA Certifications." National Court Reporters Association. Retrieved January 15, 2016 (http://www.ncra.org/Certifications/content.cfm?ItemNumber=8657&).

O'Connor, Shawn P. "How to Best Prepare for the LSAT." US News, April 23, 2012. Retrieved January 15, 2016 (http://www.usnews.com/education/blogs/law-admissions-lowdown/2012/04/23/how-to-best-prepare-for-the-lsat.).

"Paralegal Internship." ParalegelEdu.org. Retrieved January 16, 2016 (http://www.paralegaledu.org/paralegal-internship).

"Preparing for the LSAT." Law School Admission Council. Retrieved January 15, 2016 (http://www.lsac.org/jd/lsat/ preparing-for-the-lsat).

"State Interpreter Certification." National Center for State Courts. Retrieved January 15, 2016 (http://www.ncsc. org/Education-and-Careers/State-Interpreter- Certification.aspx).

"Types of Lawyers." LawyerEdu.org. Retrieved January 10, 2016 (http://www.lawyeredu.org/law-careers.html).

Vorro, Alex. "Mentoring helps attorneys at all levels advance their careers." Inside Counsel, March 27, 2012. Retrieved January 15, 2016 (http://www.insidecounsel. com/2012/03/27/ mentoring-helps-attorneys-at-all-levels-advance-th).

"What Types of Careers Are in the Field of Law?" Chron. com. Retrieved January 10, 2016 (http://work.chron.com/ types-careers-field-law-15265.html).

Zaretsky, Staci. "Which State Has the Most Difficult Bar Exam?" Above the Law. Retrieved January 16, 2016 (http://abovethelaw.com/2013/04/ which-state-has-the-most-difficult-bar-exam).

A

accounting, 26
arbitrators, 19, 54
assistant secretaries, 33
associate's degree, 42

B

bachelor's degree, 24, 28, 42
bankruptcy, 12
bar exams, 30–31, 49–50
bookkeeping, 26
budgeting, 26, 48
business law, 50

C

CareerBuilder, 34
certificate programs, 24, 26, 28, 63
civil law, 50
civil rights, 10, 53
civil unions, 11
community colleges, 44, 46
computer skills, 26, 58
constitutional law, 50
copyright, 12, 37, 58
corporate law, 8, 10, 28, 33, 37
court clerks, 44, 51, 53, 67
court interpreters, 19, 39, 44, 54, 58
court reporters, 19, 44
criminal law, 7–8, 11, 28, 50

E

electronic discovery experts, 19, 58
employment agencies, 56–57
employment law, 10
entry-level jobs, 33, 67
environmental law, 10
estate law, 12
ethics, 64

F

family law, 11, 28, 50, 58
file clerks, 7, 19, 24, 53, 54
first day on the job, 62–64
five-year plans, 58

G

good impression, making a, 60–61
guidance counselors, 32, 39

H

high school diploma, 22
human resources, 62

I

immigration law, 11
Indeed, 34
international law, 14
internships, 4, 32, 37–38, 39, 44

J

job interviews, 32, 51–61
jobs, researching, 5–6, 32–41
judges, 6, 18, 19, 21, 67
Juris Doctor (J.D.) degree, 29, 30, 31
jurists, 19
jury consultants, 19, 58

L

labor law, 10
law libraries, 48
Lawmatch, 33, 34
law school, 4, 6, 22, 28–31, 47, 48, 50, 58
Law School Admission Test (LSAT), 29, 46, 47, 48
legal analysts, 19, 24
legal assistants, 7, 16, 24, 26, 31
legal secretaries, 33, 44, 53, 58, 64
litigation support consultants, 19

M

mediators, 19
mentors, 4, 37, 38–39, 41
Microsoft Excel, 26
Multistate Bar Exam (MBE), 50

N

National Center for State Courts (NCSC), 44
National Court Reporters Association (NCRA), 44

P

paralegals, 4, 6, 7, 16, 18, 24, 28, 31, 37, 44, 64, 67
pleas, 16
private practice, 6
prosecutors, 64
public service, 6

R

real estate law, 11, 50
recommendations, getting, 41
recruitment websites, 33
resumes, 6, 34, 39, 57

S

securities law, 8, 10
sports/entertainment law, 12
stenographers, 19, 24, 39, 42, 53, 54, 61, 64
study groups, 46
study guides, 46–47
study methods, 45
subpoenas, 16

About the Author

Kathy Furgang has written dozens of books for young readers, including books for teens about breaking into sports law, getting internships, and choosing a vo-tech track for success in business. She graduated from Fordham University and now writes full time in the education market. She lives in upstate New York with her husband and two sons.

Photo Credits

Cover, p. 1 (figure) Dean Mitchell/Vetta/Getty Images; cover, p. 1 (background) Gary Hofheimer/Photolibrary/Getty Images; p. 5 Richard Cummins/Lonely Planet Images/Getty Images; pp. 8-9 Fuse/Getty Images; p. 13 Epoxydude/Getty Images; pp. 14-15 Gina Ferazzi/Los Angeles Times/Getty Images; pp. 17, 26-27, 66 Dave & Les Jacobs/Blend Images/Getty Images; p. 20, 68 Paul Bradbury/Caiaimage/Getty Images; pp. 23, 34-35 VStock LLC/Tanya Constantine/Getty Images; p. 25 Image Source/Photodisc/Getty Images; p. 30 Lane V. Erickson/Shutterstock.com; p. 33 Steve Debenport/E+/Getty Images; p. 36 © NetPhotos/Alamy Stock Photo; pp. 40-41 Hero Images/Getty Images; p. 43 Daniel Grill/Getty Images; p. 45 Spencer Weiner/Los Angeles Times/Getty Images; p. 47 rafal/E+/Getty Images; p. 49 Bloomberg/Getty Images; p. 52 Piotr Powietrzynski/age fotostock/Getty Images; pp. 54-55 Multi-bits/Stone/Getty Images; pp. 56-57 GlobalStock/E+/Getty Images; p. 59 Martin Barraud/Iconica/Getty Images; p. 60 Caiaimage/Getty Images p. 65 Robert Daly/Caiaimage/Getty Images; interior pages background image Nirat.pix/Shutterstock.com

Designer: Nicole Russo; Editor: Philip Wolny;
Photo Researcher: Philip Wolny